Dad

Christine Finochio • Jennette MacKenzie

Look!

Dad is waking up.

Look!

Dad is shaving.

Look!

Dad is cooking breakfast.

Look!

Dad is going to work.

Look!

Dad is shopping.

Look!

Dad is playing.

Look!

Dad is cleaning up.

Look!

Dad is sleeping.